17

ANTARCTICA

Sally Morgan & Pauline Lalor

SIMON & SCHUSTER
YOUNG BOOKS

Our planet has many different environments in which a rich variety of plants and animals make their homes. These environments are unique, but they are all under threat — from the growing human population, its industry and its pollution. Young readers can't protect fragile environments unless they understand them. The Living World gives insight into these special areas and makes positive suggestions for their future management.

Commissioning editor: Daphne Butler
Book editor: Claire Llewellyn
Design and artwork: SPL Design
Photographs: Ecoscene, except
Zefa (21bl, 24, 25)
Typesetting and layout: Quark Xpress

First published in Great Britain in 1992
by Simon & Schuster Young Books

Simon & Schuster Young Books
Campus 400, Maylands Avenue
Hemel Hempstead, Herts HP2 7EZ

© 1992 Simon & Schuster Young Books

Printed and bound in Portugal
by Edições ASA

A catalogue record for this book
is available from the British Library
ISBN 0 7500 1096 7

(Opposite title page)
A penguin rookery: many scientists visit
Antarctica to study the wildlife.

Contents

What is Antarctica?   6-7
A land of ice   8-9
Summers and winters   10-11
Plant life   12-13
Animals in the cold   14-15
Food in the oceans   16-17
Birds in Antarctica   18-19
Emperor penguins   20-21
Antarctic seals   22-23
Magnificent whales   24-25
People in Antarctica   26-27
Planning the future   28-29

Index   30

What is Antarctica?

Antarctica is not a country. It's a whole continent—a huge area of land like Europe or Africa.

Where is it?

The Antarctic is at the very southern-most part of the world— what we call the South Pole. It is enormous, bigger than Europe and USA together, and separated from the rest of the world by vast stormy oceans.

◄ *Mountainous islands in Antarctica.*

A rare view: Antarctica spreads across the southern-most part of the world. ▼

What is it like?

It is the coldest and windiest place on Earth. Nearly all the ground is covered by a thick layer of ice. Days and nights are very different in Antarctica during the course of a year. In the middle of winter the days are as dark as the nights. In mid-summer, the nights are as light as the days.

Can living things survive in an environment like this? Are there any animals or plants that have found ways to cope with the extreme cold and wind?

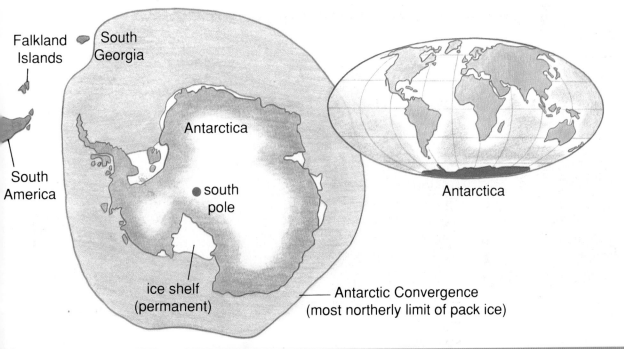

Falkland Islands

South Georgia

South America

Antarctica

south pole

ice shelf (permanent)

Antarctic Convergence (most northerly limit of pack ice)

Antarctica

A land of ice

Antarctica is a very mountainous land, with some of the highest mountains in the world. However, most of them cannot be seen because they are buried under a thick layer of ice. The ice sheet was formed by snow building up over millions of years, filling the valleys and covering the mountains. In some places it s more than four kilometres thick.

Huge icebergs break away from the ice sheet and drift out to sea.▼

Icebergs

Along the coast of Antarctica white cliffs of ice tower above the sea. From time to time, huge chunks of ice break off from the cliffs and float away. They are called icebergs and they can be huge—the size of a small town. They may drift for thousands of kilometres before melting completely.

Frozen seas

Ice is lighter than water and will float, just like ice cubes in a drink. An Antarctic winter is so cold that the whole surface of the sea freezes and floats on the water below. The floating ice is called pack ice, and it extends far out from the land for hundreds of kilometres.

Old and new pack ice: much of the pack ice thaws during the summer months, but freezes over again as the winter returns. ▶

The pack ice forms a frozen sheet over the sea. ▼

▲ During the winter months the South Pole is tilted away from the sun. Because of this, the sun never rises above the horizon, and the only light comes from the moon and stars.

Dark winters

In winter, Antarctica is the most unwelcoming place on Earth. The sun never rises, so it is dark all day long. The only light comes from the stars and moon. With no sun to warm the land, the temperature is very, very cold, falling as much as 70°C below freezing.

What is the temperature inside a kitchen freezer? Is it colder, or warmer, than the Antarctic?

Light summers

In the Antarctic, the mid-summer sun shines all day and all night. However, the sun is very low in the sky and gives little warmth. Much of the warmth it does give is reflected back off the dazzling snow. Even in summer, the weather is bitterly cold. In fact, to us, it would seem like a very cold winter.

In mid-summer, when the South Pole is tilted towards the sun, the Antarctic nights are as light as the days. This photograph was taken at midnight. ➤

Strong winds

Temperatures on the coast of Antarctica are a little higher than they are inland. Here, though, the winds are very strong, reaching speeds of up to 180 kilometres per hour. Everything *feels* much colder because of the chilling effect of the wind. How does the speed of the Antarctic wind compare with the speed you usually travel in a car?

▲ *Strong winds lift the seawater into chilling walls of spray.*

When do the plants grow?

Millions of years ago the Earth's climate was much warmer than it is today. There was no ice in Antarctica, and the land was covered by plants.

It is very different now. There are few signs of plants. Plants need light and warmth, and can only grow on land where there is no ice. During the Antarctic winter there is no sunlight and the cold is beyond imagination. The plants found here grow only in the few short months of summer.

What kinds of plant?

There are no flowering plants in Antarctica. Only the simplest kind of plant can survive—plants like algae, mosses and some strange plants called liverworts. Fungi and lichens also grow here. There is such a small amount of soil, that none of these plants has proper roots. Somehow they are able to grow on the surface of rocks.

All the plants grow very slowly here in Antarctica.

▲ *Orange and yellow lichens grow on many of the rocks in Antarctica.*

Larger plants grow on the islands further north, where it is less cold. ►

Where the ice melts in the summer, a few tough grasses manage to grow between the sunny rocks.

The layers of feathers on a penguin's body keep the warmth inside and stop it escaping into the cold air.

Living at very low temperatures causes problems for animals. If any part of their body freezes, it will be badly damaged. When water freezes in a pipe, it expands and the pipe bursts, so imagine what would happen to an animal if the water in its body froze! The animals which live in Antarctica have all adapted to the cold. They have all found ways of keeping their bodies warm.

Beating the cold

Most of the animals keep warm by having some form of insulation around their body which stops their body heat from escaping. Birds, for example, have many layers of feathers, which trap the heat like the feathers in a snug duvet. Seals have a thick layer of fat called blubber below their fur, which helps to keep them warm in the icy seas. Whales spend all their time in the water and are never warmed by the sun, so they have a particularly thick layer of blubber.

▲ Under their fur, seals have a thick layer of fat—a perfect insulation against the cold.

◄ Birds, like this sheathbill, fluff out their feathers and trap warm air.

Ice fish

The fish in the seas around Antarctica have also adapted to survive the cold. One type of fish called an ice fish has a chemical in its blood which acts like an anti-freeze. It stops its blood from freezing in low temperatures.

▲ *The black-browed albatross spends much of its life flying over the ocean in search of food.*

Unlike the plants, which live on land, the animals in Antarctica can all move between both land and sea.

A warmer place

For much of the year, the seas around Antarctica are warmer than the land because they mix with warmer water from other parts of the world. Also, the salt in seawater stops it from freezing as easily as the fresh water on land. Have you ever used salt on an icy path in winter?

Plenty of oxygen

All water contains oxygen, a gas that animals and plants need in order to live. When water is cold, however, it contains even more oxygen than usual, and many living things can survive in it. The cold seas around Antarctica are very rich in oxygen, and in the summer months millions of tiny plants and animals drift in the water. They are called plankton.

The food chain

Plants can make their own food by using sunlight, but animals can't—they have to eat plants or other animals in order to survive. In the Antarctic seas, tiny plants are eaten by small shrimp-like animals called krill; the krill are eaten by whales and fish; fish are eaten by seals and seabirds. This is called a food chain.

The oceans around Antarctica are full of krill. Stormy weather washes the krill up onto beaches in huge quantities.▼

Since much of Antarctica is covered with ice, and provides little or no food, most of the birds which live here are fish-eating seabirds. The seas are full of food, and there are few predators because of the severe cold.

What kinds of bird?

There are more petrels and penguins in Antarctica than any other kind of bird.

Petrels are long-winged birds that fly low and fast over the sea skimming the surface as their beaks scoop krill from the water.

Penguins are different from most birds because they cannot fly. Their wings have no flight feathers and they waddle about on two feet. In the sea, however, they can move very fast using their wings as paddles. Their main predators are the fierce leopard seals and skuas, powerful birds which swoop down and steal the small penguin chicks.

One of the largest seabirds in the world is the albatross. These birds glide above the oceans on their huge wings. They come to Antarctica in search of food and to breed.

◄ *The penguin parent feeds on the fish it catches in the sea. It then 'coughs' fish up into its mouth and the chick feeds on it.*

▲ *The strong hooked beak of the skua helps it to catch and eat its prey— young penguins.*

◄ *Like the penguin, the albatross feeds its growing chick on small fish which it 'coughs up' from its stomach.*

The breeding season

The climate plays an important part in the life of the birds. Most of them lay their eggs in early summer when the seas are full of plankton and krill. This provides plenty of food for the young birds. They need to grow quickly in order to be large enough to survive the long, cold winter.

Breeding in winter

Emperor penguins feed all summer and are very fit and fat before they mate in the dark months of autumn. At the beginning of winter the female penguin lays one egg which she gives to the male to keep warm until it hatches. This is called incubation.

The mother then waddles across the ice and spends the next three months in the sea. Meanwhile the father balances the large egg on his feet under a fold of skin, and huddles together with other male penguins to keep warm.

At a height of just over a metre, the emperor penguin is the largest of all the penguins. It lives in very large rookeries with thousands of other penguins and is the only animal to survive the harsh winter in the middle of Antarctica.

Food for the chick

Soon after the egg hatches, the mother returns from the sea with her stomach full of fish. She 'coughs up' the food into her mouth, and the chick feeds on it. For the rest of the long, dark winter the parents take it in turns to return to the sea to get more food while the other stays with the chick.

▲ *Penguins have no flight feathers and cannot fly. They waddle over the ice sheet on two feet.*

In the sea, they use their wings as paddles. Parents take turns to catch fish for the chick. ▶

The other parents huddle together to keep themselves warm. ▼

The long winter ends

As the weather gets warmer and the days get longer, the pack ice begins to melt, and soon the sea is near enough for the chick to swim and feed itself. It must now eat enough food to be able to survive its first winter alone.

There is so much food in the sea around Antarctica that more than half of all the seals in the world live here. They are found in the oceans and on the shores of the islands which surround Antarctica. Although they spend much of their time in the water, seals have to go ashore to give birth to their young.

On land and sea

Seals are clumsy on land. They have to drag themselves across the ice, but in the sea they are transformed into graceful swimmers. Their bodies are strong and streamlined and their powerful flippers help them to swim and dive for fish and other animals to eat.

◄ *The elephant seal spends much of its life at sea but comes ashore to moult and breed.*

▲ *The leopard seal's wide mouth and sharp teeth help to make it an expert hunter.*

Crabs, elephants and leopards!

There are several different kinds of seals in Antarctica and the most common is the crab eater. It does not actually eat crabs, as its name suggests, but feeds on krill which it sieves through its mouth.

The leopard seal is a hunter. It is the fastest swimmer and catches penguins as well as fish and krill.

The largest of the seals is the elephant seal. Like other seals, they come ashore to breed. The males are very aggressive and frighten off rival males by roaring at them and blowing up their nose just like a balloon. If this fails they will fight each other.

Whales are the largest animals in the world. Like seals and penguins, they are streamlined for swimming and have a thick layer of blubber to keep them warm.

Large mouths, small food

Although whales are huge, many of them feed on the plankton and krill that drift in the seawater. They manage to catch such tiny food by filtering the water through huge sieves, inside their mouths, called baleen. Whales swim with their mouths open, trapping food as the seawater passes through the sieve. The killer whale, however, hunts and feeds on seals.

A humpback whale with its young. Adult humpbacks can stay under water for almost an hour before having to surface for air. ▼

Mammals like us

Whales may look like fish but they are more closely related to humans. They can't breathe under water and need to come up to the surface regularly for air. Also, they don't lay eggs like fish, but give birth like humans to a baby which feeds on its mother's milk. Like us, they are called mammals.

▲ *The open mouth of this humpback whale exposes the huge sieves, called baleen, which hang inside.*

Hunting the whales

The number of whales around Antarctica has been devastated by hunting. Whales were killed for the valuable oil which could be made from their blubber. Most whale hunting is now banned, fortunately.

Just visiting

Antarctica is so far from the rest of the world that no people ever came to live here permanently. Even today, few people live in Antarctica because the weather is too severe, and there are few ice-free places where towns could be built. Most of the people who visit Antarctica are scientists and some stay for many months.

▲ *Scientists have built small settlements of huts and shelters on the coast, but only a few people stay here all year round.*

They come from all over the world to study the ice sheet and observe the wildlife. They have built camps, airstrips, and fuel stores; they use vehicles which move across the ice.

Long-lasting damage

Although most of Antarctica is still unspoilt, changes are slowly taking place. Wherever people go—even scientists— damage and pollution follow. Too many of the visiting scientists leave their rubbish lying about when they leave, and because of the severe cold, it takes years to rot. The weight of vehicles travelling over the land damages the fragile covering of plants which may take hundreds of years to grow back. Nothing changes quickly in such extreme cold. A single footprint on a patch of moss may last for many years.

These vehicles are laboratories, in which scientists study penguins, but their movements may damage the moss and other plants. ▼

The Antarctic Treaty

Antarctica is the last unspoilt continent on Earth. Its future is in the balance.

A number of countries have bases in Antarctica; these and other countries have signed a treaty, agreeing to work together peacefully.

The treaty states that no single country should ever own Antarctica and that scientists from different countries should help one another. Strict rules have been agreed about the hunting of whales, seals, and fish. No one is allowed to dump dangerous waste in Antarctica or to explode nuclear weapons there.

⬩ A scientist is about to tag an elephant seal. Only by studying animals will we learn to understand their needs.

The remarkable landscape and wildlife of Antarctica are threatened by development. How can they be preserved? ➤

What next?

Some people fear there may be hidden riches in Antarctica. The rocks under the ice sheet may contain precious metals, coal and oil. If this was true many countries would want to mine these valuable materials.

Roads, airstrips and mines would all follow, along with pollution. However, very few places are suitable for industry and the only ice-free land is used by penguins and seals. What would happen to them?

A World Park?

The Antarctic Treaty forbids mining for the next 50 years, but many people believe that the best way to protect Antarctica would be to make it the first World Park. It would be a place where there was no development, where the unique plants and animals could continue to live safely in the world's last remaining wilderness.

Let's hope so. Antarctica is too precious to spoil.

Antarctic Treaty 28, 29

birds 14, 15, 16, 17, 18, 19
blubber 14, 24, 25

coast 8, 11, 22

feathers 14, 15, 18, 21
fish 15, 17, 18, 20, 21, 22, 23, 28

ice 7, 8, 9, 12, 18, 22, 26, 30
icebergs 8
ice sheet 8, 21, 26, 28
insulation 14, 15
islands 6, 12, 22

krill 17, 18, 23, 24

mining 28, 29
mountains 7, 8

pack ice 9, 21
penguins 4, 14, 18, 19, 20, 21, 23, 24, 27, 28, 30
plankton 16, 19, 24
plants 7, 12, 16, 17, 27, 28, 30
pollution 27, 28
predators 18, 23

scientists 4, 26, 27, 28
sea 7, 8, 9, 11, 14, 15, 16, 17, 18, 20, 21, 22
seals 14, 15, 17, 18, 22, 23, 24, 28, 30
South Pole 7, 10
summer 7, 9, 10, 12, 19, 20
sun 10, 14

whales 14, 17, 24, 25, 28
wind 7, 11
winter 7, 9, 10, 12, 19, 20, 21

An Antarctic landscape—with a crabeater seal, emperor penguins, and long shadows across the ice. ➤